PLANNING YOUR LIFE TO THE

52nd Power
PLANNER+

By Danese Banks

Copyright © 2023 Danese Banks

All rights reserved. In accordance with U.S. Copyright Act of 1976, the scanning, uploading, and electronic sharing of any part of this book without permission of the publisher constitute unlawful piracy and theft of the author's intellectual property. No part of this book may be reproduced in any form by any electronic or mechanical means (including photocopying, recording or information storage and retrieval) without permission in writing from the author or publisher. Thank you for your support of the author's rights. If you would like to purchase bulk or wholesale copies, please contact the publisher at richterpublishing@icloud.com.

Published by Richter Publishing LLC www.richterpublishing.com

Book Cover Design: Tara & Jessie

Editors: Brianna Miranda-Solberg

Book Formatting & Inside Graphic Design: Jessie Alarcon

ISBN: 978-1-954094-33-8

U.S. Library of Congress Registration & Copyright Number: (coming soon)

This book is dedicated to my family. To my husband, my children, my parents and my sister. For loving me, encouraging me, and supporting me both voluntarily and sometimes involuntarily, for the past several years while I wandered into my purpose. Thank you.

"All that is gold does not glitter, not all those who wander are lost; the old that is strong does not wither, deep roots are not reached by the frost."
- J. R. R. Tolkien

"But they who wait for the Lord shall renew their strength; they shall mount up with wings like eagles; they shall run and not be weary; they shall walk and not faint."
Isaiah 40:31

INTRODUCTION

The "Planning Your Life to the 52nd Power" Planner was actually birthed from my own experience of The Power of One Small Thing. This one thing began with a challenge I created for myself to become more comfortable with talking in front of a camera. You see, I am an attorney turned mediator and life coach. And at some point during my transition, I was asked by a local TV network to talk on the topic of New Year's Resolutions and how to keep them. This was in 2021 in the midst of the pandemic.

At the time, although I had been an attorney for 20 plus years and had tried many cases in front of a jury, I was still by nature...shy, especially in front of a camera. So, I decided to prepare myself for a 3-5 minute interview in front of the camera by spending hours on zoom recording and practicing what I was going to say. Once I did that and realized it was NOT in fact going to be the death of me, I decided I would edit that content and post it on my Facebook page. After surviving that a couple of times, I decided I would talk about other important, life changing topics on a weekly basis. This is when I had the idea for my challenge.

I challenged myself to do this 52 times. During the course of meeting my personal goal, I got the bright idea of spreading these truly life changing powers with the world in the form of a planner, so that anyone who wanted to benefit from them could do so.

You see, these powers will actually empower you to change your life in an easy and "no pressure" way. So, if you're ready, there's no time like the present....START TODAY!

Take your "power" back! Love, Denise

TODAY

This is the beginning of a new day.
I have been given this day to use as I will.
I can waste it or use it for good.
What I do with today is important,
Because I am exchanging a day of my life for it.
When tomorrow comes, this day will be gone forever,
Leaving in its place something I have traded for it.

Adapted from Dr. W. Heartsill Wilson

Personal Information Page

Name: _____

Email: _____

Home: _____

Office: _____

Cell: _____

INSTRUCTIONS

If you are a person who loves a minimalistic styled planner, one with more than enough space to write your schedule and things to do, and includes just enough content to help you develop and become your best self, this is the planner for you!

The "Planning Your Life to the 52nd Power" Planner is about intentionally picking one thing, one area, one topic to focus on each week to significantly improve the quality and enjoyment of your life.

Each week has a different power to contemplate and a few questions to consider regarding each power. The purpose is to help you focus and be mindful of how you schedule your days and spend your time so that you can experience a life change for the better!

The goal of this planner is not only to help you keep organized with your day to day activities, but to also, more importantly, assist you in incorporating these helpful life changing powers to help you truly live your best life!

I hope you enjoy this labor of love!

	SUNDAY	**MONDAY**	**TUESDAY**
MONTH			
TO-DO-LIST			
○ _____			
○ _____			
○ _____			
○ _____			
○ _____			
○ _____			
○ _____			
○ _____			
○ _____			
○ _____			

NOTES
_____
_____
_____
_____

WEDNESDAY	THURSDAY	FRIDAY	SATURDAY

NOTES

	SUNDAY	**MONDAY**	**TUESDAY**
MONTH			
TO-DO-LIST			
○ _____			
○ _____			
○ _____			
○ _____			
○ _____			
○ _____			
○ _____			
○ _____			
○ _____			
○ _____			

NOTES
_____
_____
_____
_____

WEDNESDAY	THURSDAY	FRIDAY	SATURDAY

NOTES

	SUNDAY	MONDAY	TUESDAY
MONTH			
TO-DO-LIST			

NOTES

WEDNESDAY	THURSDAY	FRIDAY	SATURDAY

NOTES
_____
_____
_____
_____

	SUNDAY	MONDAY	TUESDAY

MONTH

TO-DO-LIST

- _____
- _____
- _____
- _____
- _____
- _____
- _____
- _____
- _____
- _____

NOTES

WEDNESDAY	THURSDAY	FRIDAY	SATURDAY

NOTES

	SUNDAY	MONDAY	TUESDAY

MONTH

TO-DO-LIST

_____
_____
_____
_____
_____
_____
_____
_____
_____
_____
_____
_____

NOTES

_____   _____
_____   _____
_____   _____
_____   _____

WEDNESDAY	THURSDAY	FRIDAY	SATURDAY

NOTES

MONTH

TO-DO-LIST

	SUNDAY	MONDAY	TUESDAY

NOTES

WEDNESDAY	THURSDAY	FRIDAY	SATURDAY

NOTES

	SUNDAY	MONDAY	TUESDAY
MONTH			
TO-DO-LIST			

NOTES

WEDNESDAY	THURSDAY	FRIDAY	SATURDAY

NOTES

	SUNDAY	MONDAY	TUESDAY

MONTH

TO-DO-LIST

- _____
- _____
- _____
- _____
- _____
- _____
- _____
- _____
- _____
- _____

NOTES

WEDNESDAY	THURSDAY	FRIDAY	SATURDAY

NOTES

MONTH

TO-DO-LIST

	SUNDAY	MONDAY	TUESDAY

NOTES

WEDNESDAY	THURSDAY	FRIDAY	SATURDAY

NOTES

| | **SUNDAY** | **MONDAY** | **TUESDAY** |

MONTH

TO-DO-LIST

_____

_____

_____

_____

_____

_____

_____

_____

_____

NOTES

_____ _____

_____ _____

_____ _____

_____ _____

WEDNESDAY	THURSDAY	FRIDAY	SATURDAY

NOTES

	SUNDAY	**MONDAY**	**TUESDAY**
MONTH			
TO-DO-LIST			

NOTES

WEDNESDAY	THURSDAY	FRIDAY	SATURDAY

NOTES

	SUNDAY	**MONDAY**	**TUESDAY**
MONTH			
TO-DO-LIST			
○ _____			
○ _____			
○ _____			
○ _____			
○ _____			
○ _____			
○ _____			
○ _____			
○ _____			
○ _____			

NOTES
_____ _____
_____ _____
_____ _____

WEDNESDAY	THURSDAY	FRIDAY	SATURDAY

NOTES

The Power of ONE SMALL THING

The Power of
ONE SMALL THING

The Power of One Small Thing is about how doing just one small thing can make a big difference in your life.

> We often believe that we must make a big change or carry out a long list of things to make a difference, but that simply is not true.

For example, one small thing we could do differently is going to bed an hour earlier.

> Going to bed an hour earlier could lead to us getting up and feeling refreshed, which could lead to us not rushing in the morning to get ready and we could avoid being cranky. All of this could lead to us having a greater morning with our family and ourselves, which could lead to a more productive and happier day at our job.

All because of one teeny, tiny thing.

> What's the one small thing that you could do this week that could make a huge difference in your life?

Week of

_____

QUESTIONS TO CONSIDER

1. How did I apply this power this week?

2. How was my life changed/improved/better for using this power?

3. How will I move forward with this particular power?

NOTES

SUNDAY

MONDAY

TUESDAY

WEDNESDAY

TO-DO-LIST

THURSDAY

FRIDAY

SATURDAY

I am using the **POWER** of
One Small Thing

The Power of
DECLARATION

The Power of DECLARATION

Power 2

The Power of Declaration is about recognizing the importance of your words and using them in a positive and powerful way.

Often times, we are using our words in a way that is negative and only further allows us to experience negative outcomes.

This happens when we complain or allow our inner critic to take hold of our thoughts.

Instead, we should direct our energy regarding ourselves, our family, and our friends in a more positive direction.

This week, allow yourself to make positive declarations over your life.

A good one I learned from Joel Osteen's book, I Declare: 31 Promises to Speak Over Your Life is, "I declare God's dream for my life is coming to pass. It will not be stopped by people, disappointments or adversities. God has solutions to every problem I will ever face already lined up. The right people and the right breaks are in my future. I will fulfill my destiny."

You can create your own declaration of course, but if you don't have one, this is a great place to start. Start today. What's your declaration for this week?

Week of
_____

QUESTIONS TO CONSIDER

1 How did I apply this power this week?

2 How was my life changed/improved/better for using this power?

3 How will I move forward with this particular power?

NOTES

| ____ | **SUNDAY** |

| ____ | **MONDAY** |

| ____ | **TUESDAY** |

| ____ | **WEDNESDAY** |

TO-DO-LIST

THURSDAY

FRIDAY

SATURDAY

I am using the **POWER** of **Declaration**

The Power of BABY STEPS

The Power of
BABY STEPS

Power 3

A dream written down with a date becomes a goal.

> A goal broken down into steps becomes a plan.

A plan backed by action makes your dream come true.

> A lot of us have dreams that didn't come to fruition because we didn't make those dreams goals.

And a lot of us have goals that we didn't meet because we didn't sit down and make a plan.

> A lot of us also have plans that didn't move forward because we didn't take baby steps to make the plan doable.

This is why baby steps are so important. They are the catalyst of making our dreams come true.

> You can also apply the concept of baby steps to handling your problems.

Which way will you use baby steps this week? Will you solve a problem with it or move closer toward one of your dreams?

Week of

_____

QUESTIONS TO CONSIDER

1. How did I apply this power this week?

2. How was my life changed/improved/better for using this power?

3. How will I move forward with this particular power?

NOTES

SUNDAY

MONDAY

TUESDAY

WEDNESDAY

TO-DO-LIST

THURSDAY

FRIDAY

SATURDAY

I am using the **POWER** of **Baby Steps**

The Power of
AVOIDING THE DOWNWARD SPIRAL

The Power of
AVOIDING THE DOWNWARD SPIRAL

Power 4

The Downward Spiral is when something happens in our life that we do not like or that was bad, and we continue to build upon it with one bad or negative thing after another, until we don't even recognize how we got there.

> I am not talking about true depression or when obvious horrible things happen like we lose our job or have a death in the family, etc.

I am talking about the smaller negative things that happen, that we then allow to cloud our entire being.

> A small example could be that we are driving to work and someone flips us off. And then before we know it, we are cussing them out. Which leads to a bad drive into work. Which leads to us being in a grumpy mood and having a less than productive or happy day. Because now we are looking at everything that occurs through the filter of the feeling we felt as we drove into work.

The trick to dealing with and ultimately avoiding the downward spiral is this: When we find ourselves thinking, "nothing good is happening to me" and "why is everything going wrong," we need to take a pause and really examine our situation.

> Is everything as bad as we believe it to be or are we making it worse in our heads?

Because if we are just making it bad and horrible in our heads, we can change it; we can turn it around.

> And if it is really that bad, we can apply what we learned about baby steps and deal with the problem accordingly.

If you find yourself going down the rabbit hole of negativity this week, what is one way that you can apply this power to your life?

Week of
_____

QUESTIONS TO CONSIDER

1. How did I apply this power this week?

2. How was my life changed/improved/better for using this power?

3. How will I move forward with this particular power?

NOTES

	SUNDAY
___	

	MONDAY
___	

	TUESDAY
___	

	WEDNESDAY
___	

TO-DO-LIST

THURSDAY

FRIDAY

SATURDAY

I am using the **POWER** of
Avoiding the Downward Spiral

The Power of CHANCE

The Power of
CHANCE

Power 5

Chances are often opportunities in disguise that we often let pass us by because we are afraid.

> We often go back to some past hurt we experienced when we took a chance and things didn't go our way; and then, we apply that one time to everything that comes our way in the future.

Stop doing that.

> Instead of playing the "what if" game of everything that could go wrong, play the "what if" game of everything going right, or even better than we could imagine.

What if it works out? What if it presents a huge opportunity?

> This week, be very intentional about the chances that come your way. Don't let fear prevent you from experiencing something beautiful and meaningful that might just change your life.

Take a chance on something (nothing crazy, risky, or illegal, of course). But take a chance on something new, something different, and you'll be glad you did.

Week of

_____

QUESTIONS TO CONSIDER

1. How did I apply this power this week?

2. How was my life changed/improved/better for using this power?

3. How will I move forward with this particular power?

NOTES

SUNDAY

MONDAY

TUESDAY

WEDNESDAY

TO-DO-LIST

THURSDAY

FRIDAY

SATURDAY

I am using the **POWER** of

Chance

The Power of
LOVE

The Power of LOVE

Power 6

Love is a concept we can all easily grasp. There is always someone that we show love to, whether it's our friends, our family members, or even our fur babies.

> We'll move mountains, cross oceans, experience all kinds of hardship for those that we hold near and dear to our hearts.

Think about that feeling for a moment, how strong and powerful it is.

> Relish in how good it feels to love someone.

Now, I want you to apply that same love to....yourself.

> How many of us shortchange ourselves in the love department?

If you are someone who shows yourself that same magnitude of love that you show others, great! Keep doing it.

> But if you are someone that struggles with it, use this week, the next week, and the one after that to be intentional about showing yourself love.

Love yourself just as much as you love everybody else this week.

Week of

_____

QUESTIONS TO CONSIDER

1 How did I apply this power this week?

2 How was my life changed/improved/better for using this power?

3 How will I move forward with this particular power?

NOTES

| _____ | **SUNDAY** |

| _____ | **MONDAY** |

| _____ | **TUESDAY** |

| _____ | **WEDNESDAY** |

TO-DO-LIST

THURSDAY

FRIDAY

SATURDAY

I am using the **POWER** of
Love

The Power of
PARTNERSHIP

The Power of PARTNERSHIP

Power 7

The Power of Partnership refers to more than just romantic relationships.

What I am referring to is how we partner with others to either become our best versions of ourselves or our worst versions.

How often have you had a great idea and told a friend about it, who in return told you it was dumb or stupid? Before you knew it, you then also thought your idea was dumb or stupid. Did you think your idea was dumb or stupid before you shared it? If not, this is an example of partnering with someone, and you probably weren't even aware of it.

Or how many of us believe we can do all things by ourselves and refuse to partner with someone that could support us or expedite what we are trying to accomplish?

Both of these are examples of how The Power of Partnership works- both in a positive and negative way.

Are you partnering with someone right now? If not, should you be? If you are, is it working for you? Either way, put some thought into it this week and decide if this is an area in which you might consider making a change.

Week of
_____

QUESTIONS TO CONSIDER

1. How did I apply this power this week?

2. How was my life changed/improved/better for using this power?

3. How will I move forward with this particular power?

NOTES

_____	**SUNDAY**

_____	**MONDAY**

_____	**TUESDAY**

_____	**WEDNESDAY**

TO-DO-LIST

THURSDAY

FRIDAY

SATURDAY

I am using the **POWER** of **Partnership**

The Power of
COMMUNICATION AND COMPREHENSION

The Power of
COMMUNICATION AND COMPREHENSION

Power 8

Most people recognize the importance of communication. However, communication is nothing if comprehension is not present, as well.

> Being a good communicator is about conveying your feelings in the best way that you can, with an attempt to speak in a way that you believe is as clear as possible.

But comprehension is taking the extra step to be assured that the person listening truly understands what you are trying to convey.

> A lot of times, we don't take that extra step and then get upset when someone doesn't understand us or doesn't do what we thought they would, even though we believe we communicated with them clearly.

In order to use this power to the fullest, particularly when having difficult discussions with people, do your best to communicate your feelings to them.

> Then take the extra step of asking them to reframe or repeat what you said, to make sure they understand you.
> Taking the extra step on the front end can prevent a lot of misunderstanding on the back end.

If you plan on having a regular or even difficult conversation with someone this week, how will you incorporate this power into your discussion?

Week of

_____

QUESTIONS TO CONSIDER

1. How did I apply this power this week?

2. How was my life changed/improved/better for using this power?

3. How will I move forward with this particular power?

NOTES

SUNDAY

MONDAY

TUESDAY

WEDNESDAY

TO-DO-LIST

THURSDAY

FRIDAY

SATURDAY

I am using the **POWER** of **Communication and Comprehension**

The Power of
GRACE AND MERCY

The Power of
GRACE AND MERCY

Power 9

The Power of Grace and Mercy is about giving ourselves and each other permission to be human.

> It's about acknowledging that we all make mistakes, and because we know that, we can give ourselves a pass when we mess up from time to time.

Often, when we or someone else messes up, we can be so hard on ourselves or them.

> We become judgmental when it comes to others; we start bullying ourselves when it comes to us.

Neither reaction is necessary.

> Instead, take a pause, step back, and acknowledge either your own humanity or theirs.

And extend to yourself and others something that God gives us daily, grace and mercy.

> This week, try extending grace and mercy to either yourself or others and watch how your life can change for the better.

Week of
_____

QUESTIONS TO CONSIDER

1. How did I apply this power this week?

2. How was my life changed/improved/better for using this power?

3. How will I move forward with this particular power?

NOTES

SUNDAY

MONDAY

TUESDAY

WEDNESDAY

TO-DO-LIST

THURSDAY

FRIDAY

SATURDAY

I am using the **POWER** of **Grace and Mercy**

The Power of
INTUITION

The Power of
INTUITION

Power 10

Most of us spend a lot of time asking others for their advice and opinions without really digging deep and figuring out what we think about a particular situation.

> But if we took the time to really listen to ourselves, we would find that we already know what's best for us in any given situation.

It's that little voice in our heads, not the one that plays the "what if" game with us and gets us all anxious and fearful.
It's the gut feeling we have, the instincts, the belief in ourselves that we just won't trust.

> This week, trust you. Trust your intuition. Trust that little voice.

Make at least one decision without consulting others and see what happens.

> And when it turns out well for you, start listening to it more and more.

Week of

_____

QUESTIONS TO CONSIDER

1. How did I apply this power this week?

2. How was my life changed/improved/better for using this power?

3. How will I move forward with this particular power?

NOTES

| ____ | **SUNDAY** |

| ____ | **MONDAY** |

| ____ | **TUESDAY** |

| ____ | **WEDNESDAY** |

TO-DO-LIST

THURSDAY

FRIDAY

SATURDAY

I am using the **POWER** of
Intuition

The Power of
SHIFTING YOUR MINDSET

The Power of SHIFTING YOUR MINDSET

Power 11

This is a very important power as it has such a huge effect on all kinds of things.

> The Power of Shifting Your Mindset is choosing to look at a situation, good or bad, in a way that is helpful to you.

Your mindset about a situation can either make you or break you.

> Therefore, choosing to look at it and experience it in a way that you can get something out of the experience, makes all the difference.

It's more than just positive thinking or seeing the glass half full.

> It's about truly practicing opportunistic thinking in which you are able to take nearly any event that happens to you, and see what you can learn from it, how you can grow from it, and be better because of the experience.

This week, especially if you feel stuck or stagnant or upset about a particular situation, see how you can shift your mindset and look at it through a different filter.

Week of
_____

QUESTIONS TO CONSIDER

1 How did I apply this power this week?

2 How was my life changed/improved/better for using this power?

3 How will I move forward with this particular power?

NOTES

____ SUNDAY

____ MONDAY

____ TUESDAY

____ WEDNESDAY

TO-DO-LIST

THURSDAY

FRIDAY

SATURDAY

I am using the **POWER** of **Shifting Your Mindset**

The Power of
DECIDING

The Power of DECIDING

Power 12

The Power of Deciding is about moving forward in making a decision.

> A lot of times we go back and forth and procrastinate.

Is choosing "A" better than "B"? Is choosing "B" better than "A"? Sometimes we ponder things for so long that we do not make a decision at all.

> And even not making a decision is problematic because we did not exert control over the outcome when we had a chance to.

And now we are stuck with whatever happens.

> Making the wrong decision is even better than no decision at all.

A lot of times, even when making the wrong decision, we are able to backtrack or tweak it for a better outcome.

> Don't let your fear of making the wrong decision prevent you from making one at all.

What is something this week that you have been on the fence about? Why? Decide already.

Week of

_____

QUESTIONS TO CONSIDER

1. How did I apply this power this week?

2. How was my life changed/improved/better for using this power?

3. How will I move forward with this particular power?

NOTES

SUNDAY

MONDAY

TUESDAY

WEDNESDAY

TO-DO-LIST

THURSDAY

FRIDAY

SATURDAY

I am using the **POWER** of
Deciding

TO-DO-LIST

The Power of
COURAGE

The Power of COURAGE

Power 13

Find your courage muscle and exercise it.

Often, we don't move forward in life out of fear.

We allow fear to keep us stuck in situations and circumstances that we desperately want to change or rid ourselves of completely.

We are afraid that we might not do well, that people won't like us, or even that we will succeed.

Exercising your courage muscle doesn't mean that we get rid of fear completely.

It means we do whatever the thing is anyway, scared and/or excited – scared-cited.

This week, ask yourself daily, what can I do to exercise my courage muscle? What can I try? What can I ask for? What big step can I take?

Week of
_____

QUESTIONS TO CONSIDER

1 How did I apply this power this week?

2 How was my life changed/improved/better for using this power?

3 How will I move forward with this particular power?

NOTES

____ **SUNDAY**

____ **MONDAY**

____ **TUESDAY**

____ **WEDNESDAY**

TO-DO-LIST

THURSDAY

FRIDAY

SATURDAY

I am using the **POWER** of
Courage

The Power of
USING YOUR OWN RESOURCES

The Power of USING YOUR OWN RESOURCES

Power 14

You already have what you need right now to get started.

> So many times, we put off our goals and dreams waiting for one more thing, to get one more thing, or learn one more thing, or have time for one more thing.

This is so unnecessary.

> There is something right now, right at your fingertips, that you are not using.

Use what you currently have to get what you want.

> You have enough, you know enough; more importantly, you are enough.

This week, take a look at your resources, your contacts, your knowledge, all of the things you already have access to. Make a list and start there.

Week of

_____

QUESTIONS TO CONSIDER

1. How did I apply this power this week?

2. How was my life changed/improved/better for using this power?

3. How will I move forward with this particular power?

NOTES

____ **SUNDAY**

____ **MONDAY**

____ **TUESDAY**

____ **WEDNESDAY**

TO-DO-LIST

THURSDAY

FRIDAY

SATURDAY

I am using the **POWER** of
Using your Own Resources

The Power of
PLANTING SEEDS

The Power of
PLANTING SEEDS

Power 15

The Power of Planting Seeds is about doing things with the intention to grow something good, beneficial, and productive.

> Sometimes, we are not even cognizant of what we will ultimately produce and that is perfectly fine.

This planner is a flower that bloomed from a simple request from a news station to talk about New Year's resolutions back in 2021.

> If the intent is there, it will be something good that is either beneficial to us, others, or both.

We don't have to fully understand the final outcome, we just have to plant it.

> Then water it and provide sunlight, if we truly want to expedite its growth.

This week ask yourself, where are you planting seeds? Have you been watering them? Have you been giving them sunlight? And if you haven't been, what's one seed you will plant this week? Don't worry about what, how, or if it will bloom. Just plant it.

Week of

_____

QUESTIONS TO CONSIDER

1. How did I apply this power this week?

2. How was my life changed/improved/better for using this power?

3. How will I move forward with this particular power?

NOTES

SUNDAY

MONDAY

TUESDAY

WEDNESDAY

TO-DO-LIST

THURSDAY

FRIDAY

SATURDAY

I am using the **POWER** of
Planting Seeds

TO-DO-LIST

The Power of LIGHT

The Power of LIGHT

Power 16

The only thing that can overcome darkness is light.

> When you find yourself feeling sad or depressed or some other heavy feeling, you can do little things to get yourself, one step at a time, out of a downward spiral.

I am not suggesting this for those that may suffer from clinical depression and need professional help.

> However, for those who experience sadness and other feelings every now and again, try something to take you out of that dark place.

It could be as easy as standing in the shower and letting the water run all over you or going outside and inhaling the fresh air.

> It could be as simple as watching a silly movie.

It could be as fun as spending time with someone whose energy feels like sunshine to you. Any of these examples, and countless others, can show you how The Power of Light works.

> This week, if you find yourself in a dark space or if you just want an extra boost of positive energy, try any one of the above examples or come up with one of your own and watch how quickly The Power of Light works.

Week of

_____

QUESTIONS TO CONSIDER

1. How did I apply this power this week?

2. How was my life changed/improved/better for using this power?

3. How will I move forward with this particular power?

NOTES

| _____ | **SUNDAY** |

| _____ | **MONDAY** |

| _____ | **TUESDAY** |

| _____ | **WEDNESDAY** |

TO-DO-LIST

THURSDAY

FRIDAY

SATURDAY

I am using the **POWER** of
Light

TO-DO-LIST

The Power of
CLARITY

The Power of CLARITY

Power 17

The Power of Clarity is about being clear about who we are, what we are trying to accomplish and why.

> So many people are so busy with their daily living that they never take the time to truly contemplate who they are, what they are trying to accomplish ultimately, and why.
> As a result, they are busy being busy, and nothing really changes in their lives.

Yet, they are surprised about this outcome when they've done nothing to avoid it.

> Life does not have to be this way.
> This week, cut out the distractions for whatever timeframe you can. It can be as small as 15 minutes if that's all you have.

Make a list of how you spend your time on any given day.
Make a second list of how you want to spend your time and what you want your life to look like and why.

> Now, go back and reexamine the first list. If those tasks and activities you currently engage in do not help you get closer to the life you want to have, determine which tasks and/or activities need to be deleted, delegated, or completed more efficiently to make room for the items you clearly need to reach your goals.

Week of
_____

QUESTIONS TO CONSIDER

1. How did I apply this power this week?

2. How was my life changed/improved/better for using this power?

3. How will I move forward with this particular power?

NOTES

SUNDAY
_____

MONDAY
_____

TUESDAY
_____

WEDNESDAY
_____

TO-DO-LIST

THURSDAY

FRIDAY

SATURDAY

I am using the **POWER** of
Clarity

The Power of
FOCUSING ON ONLY THE FIRST STEP

The Power of
FOCUSING ON
ONLY THE FIRST STEP

Power 18

Winter is my Siberian Husky who used to climb up our stairs at home but was afraid to go down them.

> We would try all kinds of things to get him to go downstairs, pulling him, pushing him, even trying to bribe him with his favorite treat. Nothing worked.

One day, I was trying once again to get him to come downstairs and I realized that perhaps his depth perception was off.

> Upon further evaluation, it seemed as if he was anxiously contemplating the entire staircase from the top of the steps instead of just focusing on the first step immediately in front of him.

As a result, I decided to get a big laundry basket and hide all of the steps, except the one he was about to step on.

> Amazingly this worked. Once he only had to focus on the simple task of going down the one step, he no longer had to worry about anything else.

We are a lot like Winter when we look at the entire picture of something we are trying to accomplish or even when we look at negative events.

> If we would only focus on the one task ahead, we might find that we can do both easy and hard things.

This week, reflect upon what "entire staircase" in your life you have been anxious about. Now, let's just concentrate on that first step. How does it feel to make that shift?

Week of
_____

QUESTIONS TO CONSIDER

1. How did I apply this power this week?

2. How was my life changed/improved/better for using this power?

3. How will I move forward with this particular power?

NOTES

| _____ | **SUNDAY** |

| _____ | **MONDAY** |

| _____ | **TUESDAY** |

| _____ | **WEDNESDAY** |

TO-DO-LIST

THURSDAY

FRIDAY

SATURDAY

I am using the **POWER** of **Focusing on ONLY the First Step**

The Power of
FACTS

The Power of FACTS

Power 19

Facts affect thoughts, which affect feelings, which in turn affect actions.

> When we attach our thoughts, feelings, and actions to our interpretation of a fact, we are no longer dealing with what is real and what is true.

Example: Let's say you and I are supposed to go to lunch on Tuesday, and on Monday I send you a text that says, "So sorry but I have to cancel."

> You might attach this thought to that text, "She doesn't want to eat with me."

And then you might attach a feeling of sadness and/or of anger. These feelings then lead you to avoid my calls when I call you after Tuesday.

> But was any of this real or true? Is there any other fact, other than that I texted you saying I was sorry and had to cancel?

Could I have been sick or had some sort of emergency that had nothing to do with you or our relationship?

> This week, take a look at facts, thoughts, feelings and actions and put a pause between your facts and thoughts. Consider this example to determine what is real and true and what may not be.

Week of

_____

QUESTIONS TO CONSIDER

1. How did I apply this power this week?

2. How was my life changed/improved/better for using this power?

3. How will I move forward with this particular power?

NOTES

| _____ | **SUNDAY** |

| _____ | **MONDAY** |

| _____ | **TUESDAY** |

| _____ | **WEDNESDAY** |

TO-DO-LIST

THURSDAY

FRIDAY

SATURDAY

I am using the **POWER** of

Facts

The Power of
SEPARATING YOURSELF FROM YOUR FEELINGS

The Power of
SEPARATING YOURSELF FROM YOUR FEELINGS

Power 20

It is important to realize you are not your feelings and that feelings are simply something we all experience at any given time.

> It is important to realize you are not your feelings and that feelings are simply something we all experience at any given time.

Sometimes we tend to give our feelings way too much power by expressing ourselves as being those feelings, like "I am sad" or "I am depressed."

> This causes us to feel as if those feelings have some sense of permanency about them and that they are part of our being.

This is simply not accurate.

> Feelings are fleeting. How you feel right now in this given moment, can be different 1 minute from now, 1 hour from now, 1 day, 1 week, 1 month, 1 year.

And just because you FEEL a certain way does not mean you ARE a certain way.

> This week, think about when you are feeling a certain way. Instead of saying, "I am sad" or "I am depressed," try changing that around to "I feel sad" or "I feel depressed." Remember feelings are just a temporary state of mind that you can change and control at any time you decide to.

Week of

_____

QUESTIONS TO CONSIDER

1. How did I apply this power this week?

2. How was my life changed/improved/better for using this power?

3. How will I move forward with this particular power?

NOTES

SUNDAY _____

_____
_____
_____
_____

MONDAY _____

_____
_____
_____
_____

TUESDAY _____

_____
_____
_____
_____

WEDNESDAY _____

_____
_____
_____
_____

TO-DO-LIST

THURSDAY

FRIDAY

SATURDAY

I am using the **POWER** of **Separating Yourself From Your Feelings**

The Power of
POWERFUL PAUSE

The Power of
POWERFUL PAUSE

Power 21

The Power of the Powerful Pause is the difference between you reacting to something and you responding to something.

> When something happens and we simply react, we give ourselves zero time to think about what the best way is to respond, and often we choose the wrong way.

Reacting is when you just move through life in default mode without giving any thought as to what your next step is or the consequences of your next step.

> But responding is when you insert the powerful pause and give yourself just a moment to think through your next step and DECIDE what you will do next.

There is a place for being reactive, such as when you are in survival mode and have to either take flight or fight in a given situation.

> However, most of our decisions do not have to take place with such a sense of urgency.

This week, when you have the chance to use the powerful pause, just take a moment and consciously decide the next step you will take.

Week of

_____

QUESTIONS TO CONSIDER

1. How did I apply this power this week?

2. How was my life changed/improved/better for using this power?

3. How will I move forward with this particular power?

NOTES

_____
_____
_____
_____
_____
_____
_____
_____

SUNDAY
_____
_____
_____
_____

MONDAY
_____
_____
_____
_____

TUESDAY
_____
_____
_____
_____

WEDNESDAY
_____
_____
_____
_____

TO-DO-LIST

THURSDAY

FRIDAY

SATURDAY

I am using the **POWER** of the

Powerful Pause

The Power of ENERGY

The Power of ENERGY

Power 22

The Power of Energy is about both your physical and mental energy.

> You can read about all of the other powers and understand them but you won't get anywhere if you don't have the energy to execute them.

You don't have to necessarily run to the gym to promote your physical energy, although that's great. You can just do something as simple as increasing your water intake, making sure you get enough hours of sleep, walking every other day to increase your physical energy.

> Simple steps make a difference.

In terms of mental energy, simply ridding yourselves of time or energy vampires will work wonders for you.

> A time or energy vampire is someone who literally drains your energy when you are in their presence. Sometimes, this can be a loved one, family member, friend or even co-worker.

You don't have to completely cut them off. You can set boundaries with them and how you interact with them. Protect your energy.

> This week, think of one thing you can do to increase either your mental energy or your physical energy, or even both.

Week of

_____

QUESTIONS TO CONSIDER

1. How did I apply this power this week?

2. How was my life changed/improved/better for using this power?

3. How will I move forward with this particular power?

NOTES

_____	**SUNDAY**

_____	**MONDAY**

_____	**TUESDAY**

_____	**WEDNESDAY**

TO-DO-LIST

THURSDAY

FRIDAY

SATURDAY

I am using the **POWER** of

Energy

The Power of
MOTION

The Power of MOTION

Power 23

Take a look at Newton's law of motion.

> An object at rest will stay at rest, and an object in motion will stay in motion.

Let's apply that to ourselves both physically and mentally.

> Sometimes our bodies need to rest and recharge, but there are other times when we just need to move.

We need to do something, anything. It can be as simple as getting off the couch and going outside or decluttering a small area in our homes.

> That one motion triggers us to then do another thing, and then another thing. Before you know it, we have accomplished something, either great or small.

This week, when you are feeling like doing nothing but know that you should do something, put one thing in motion, just one, and see what happens.

Week of
_____

QUESTIONS TO CONSIDER

1 How did I apply this power this week?

2 How was my life changed/improved/better for using this power?

3 How will I move forward with this particular power?

NOTES

SUNDAY

MONDAY

TUESDAY

WEDNESDAY

TO-DO-LIST

THURSDAY

FRIDAY

SATURDAY

I am using the **POWER** of
Motion

The Power of
PIVOT

The Power of PIVOT

Power 24

The Power of the Pivot is when you have a plan in place but you also have enough flexibility within your plan to make changes. Enough room to tweak or move in a completely different direction, if necessary, can make all the difference.

> It's the ability to go with the flow and not let some unforeseen or foreseen circumstance that is not within your control, mess up your ability to move forward.

Let's face it. Things happen all the time that we do not anticipate or cannot control.

> And those things affect us all the time.

When that happens, use it to your advantage as opposed to sitting back and complaining about it.

> Find the opportunity or challenge of making it work for your own good.

This week, when something happens that you didn't expect, just think about The Power of the Pivot and make that change work to your advantage.

Week of
_____

QUESTIONS TO CONSIDER

1 How did I apply this power this week?

2 How was my life changed/improved/better for using this power?

3 How will I move forward with this particular power?

NOTES

SUNDAY
_____

MONDAY
_____

TUESDAY
_____

WEDNESDAY
_____

TO-DO-LIST

THURSDAY

FRIDAY

SATURDAY

I am using the **POWER** of the

Pivot

The Power of
HAVING A TRIBE/SQUAD/CLIQUE

The Power of HAVING A TRIBE/SQUAD/CLIQUE

Power 25

The Power of Having a Tribe/Squad/Click is all about who you choose to spend time with and how they affect you.

> Your success, happiness, and peace can be linked to the people that you spend time with.

Do you spend time with people who give you energy or drain your energy?

> If they are draining your energy, spend a little more time getting to the root of that problem.

Is it them, you, or is it a combination?

> Our days are numbered and our time is short. Who you spend time with is important.

More importantly, who you spend time with is within your control. This week, think about your squad. Who's in your click? Are you spending your time wisely? If you need to make a change, just do it.

> Find people that can inspire you and motivate you and can help you on your journey as opposed to the opposite.

Week of

_____

QUESTIONS TO CONSIDER

1 How did I apply this power this week?

2 How was my life changed/improved/better for using this power?

3 How will I move forward with this particular power?

NOTES

| _____ | **SUNDAY** |

| _____ | **MONDAY** |

| _____ | **TUESDAY** |

| _____ | **WEDNESDAY** |

TO-DO-LIST

___ **THURSDAY**

___ **FRIDAY**

___ **SATURDAY**

I am using the **POWER** of
Tribe/Squad/Clique

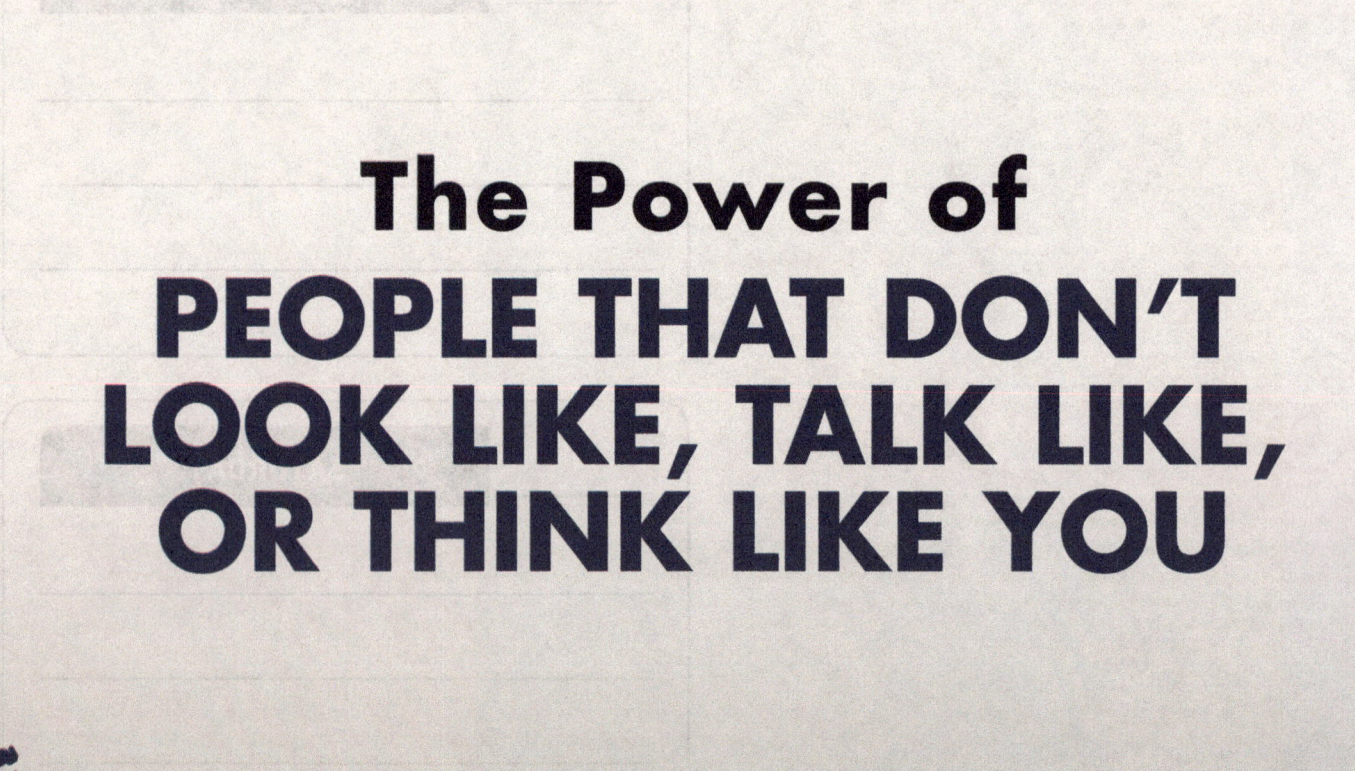

The Power of
PEOPLE THAT DON'T LOOK LIKE, TALK LIKE, OR THINK LIKE YOU

The Power of
PEOPLE THAT DON'T LOOK LIKE, TALK LIKE, OR THINK LIKE YOU

Power 26

The Power of People that Don't Look Like, Talk Like, or Think Like You is about having at least one person around you that is a friend, colleague, or family member that challenges your opinions and/or beliefs.

> While that one person may get on your nerves at times, it is necessary to have at least one person that forces you to look at something differently, even if for just a little while.

Too often, we confuse our opinions and beliefs for facts or truths simply because everyone we associate with or discuss it with thinks or believes the same way.

> This simply is not true and is a prime example of limited thinking.

This week, find someone who thinks differently from you for whatever reason, - race, religion, gender preference, politics, etc....

> Be open to a friendship or at a minimum, a "friendly discussion." You just might learn something or even change your mind about something.

Week of

_____

QUESTIONS TO CONSIDER

1. How did I apply this power this week?

2. How was my life changed/improved/better for using this power?

3. How will I move forward with this particular power?

NOTES

SUNDAY ____

MONDAY ____

TUESDAY ____

WEDNESDAY ____

TO-DO-LIST

THURSDAY

FRIDAY

SATURDAY

I am using the **POWER** of

People that Don't Look Like, Talk Like, or Think Like You

The Power of
SAYING YES

The Power of SAYING YES

Power 27

The Power of Saying Yes is for those of us who have so many boundaries around us that we won't let anyone in.

> It's for those of us who say "No!" even before others can finish asking us what they wanted.

The Power of Saying Yes is about saying "Yes!" every now and then and being willing to step out of our comfort zone and try something new.

> I am not talking about saying yes to anything dangerous, illegal or immoral.

But saying yes to something that we would normally say no to just because we haven't tried it before or because we THINK we won't like it, is not allowed.

> This week, try saying "Yes" instead of "No" at least once a day. Who knows, it could be the best experience ever!

Week of

_____

QUESTIONS TO CONSIDER

1 How did I apply this power this week?

2 How was my life changed/improved/better for using this power?

3 How will I move forward with this particular power?

NOTES

SUNDAY

MONDAY

TUESDAY

WEDNESDAY

TO-DO-LIST

THURSDAY

FRIDAY

SATURDAY

I am using the **POWER** of
Saying Yes

The Power of
SAYING NO

The Power of SAYING NO

Power 28

Unlike The Power of Saying Yes, The Power of Saying No is especially for those of us who have difficulties setting boundaries.

> There are quite a few of us who just want to please others and sometimes we do that to a fault.

The problem with this is that we can get so wrapped up in helping others and giving to others, that we neglect ourselves.

> That's where The Power of Saying No steps in.

The Power of Saying No allows you to place yourself in just as an important spot as you do others and, in fact, allows you to place your needs first.

> You don't always have to be the one to volunteer, to give in, or save the day.

This week, say no to at least three things to others and say yes to at least three things for you!

Week of

_____

QUESTIONS TO CONSIDER

1. How did I apply this power this week?

2. How was my life changed/improved/better for using this power?

3. How will I move forward with this particular power?

NOTES

_____	**SUNDAY**

_____	**MONDAY**

_____	**TUESDAY**

_____	**WEDNESDAY**

TO-DO-LIST

THURSDAY

FRIDAY

SATURDAY

I am using the **POWER** of
Saying No

The Power of
SAYING MAYBE SO

The Power of
SAYING MAYBE SO

Power 29

We cannot talk about the powers of "yes" and "no" without talking about The Power of Saying Maybe So.

> The Power of Saying Maybe So is when you need to have a delay before making a decision.

This is typically regarding big decisions that you must make, like a job change, a relocation, or even a decision to marry, have kids, or divorce.

> The Power of Saying Maybe So is when you allow yourself the time and space to truly consider a choice you have to make.

It's when you take full advantage of being in a "hallway space" of sorts and you use that limbo space and time to educate yourself and make a good decision.

> Now, the challenge of maybe so is that you can get stuck in the hallway space for too long if you are not careful. So, it is important to give yourself some sort of realistic deadline to decide, to choose and to act.

This week, think about whether there are any decisions that you need to take advantage of in a hallway space and give yourself The Power of Saying Maybe So.

Week of

_____

QUESTIONS TO CONSIDER

1. How did I apply this power this week?

2. How was my life changed/improved/better for using this power?

3. How will I move forward with this particular power?

NOTES

SUNDAY

MONDAY

TUESDAY

WEDNESDAY

TO-DO-LIST

THURSDAY

FRIDAY

SATURDAY

I am using the **POWER** of
Saying Maybe So

The Power of CELEBRATION

The Power of CELEBRATION

Power 30

The Power of Celebration is all about celebrating yourself and celebrating others. Little celebrations, big celebrations, all kinds of celebrations.

> And you don't have to wait until you get completely to the finish line or until you have something really big to talk about.

Even if it's a baby step toward one of your goals, that's a reason to celebrate.

> You can celebrate something just about every day.

In fact, the more you celebrate, the more you have to celebrate because celebration is a form of gratitude and appreciation.

> The Power of Celebration also is not just about us; it's about celebrating others as well.

This week, look for at least one thing each day to celebrate. Notice how good it feels.

Week of
_____

QUESTIONS TO CONSIDER

1 How did I apply this power this week?

2 How was my life changed/improved/better for using this power?

3 How will I move forward with this particular power?

NOTES

____	SUNDAY
____	MONDAY
____	TUESDAY
____	WEDNESDAY

TO-DO-LIST

THURSDAY

FRIDAY

SATURDAY

I am using the **POWER** of
Celebration

The Power of LAUGHTER

The Power of
LAUGHTER

Power 31

The Power of Laughter is one of the powers that is often overlooked because it's so simple.

> It's about finding something joyful in every day; it's about being able to have fun every day.

Trying to find something to laugh about or that is funny does not come easy for everyone.

> However, with a little intention placed behind this goal, you just might find it easier than you think.

Sometimes you have to trick yourself into it by watching a funny movie or listening to your favorite comedian just to get you started.

> But once you get there, it becomes easier and easier to do it and feel the joy behind this power.

I understand that life happens and sometimes it's more difficult, but when you can find laughter and joy, despite your happenstances, you're onto something truly special.

> This week, try not to take everything and everyone so seriously and try to see the fun in your everyday life. You just might find yourself a chuckle or two.

Week of

_____

QUESTIONS TO CONSIDER

1. How did I apply this power this week?

2. How was my life changed/improved/better for using this power?

3. How will I move forward with this particular power?

NOTES

| _____ | **SUNDAY** |

| _____ | **MONDAY** |

| _____ | **TUESDAY** |

| _____ | **WEDNESDAY** |

TO-DO-LIST

THURSDAY

FRIDAY

SATURDAY

I am using the **POWER** of
Laughter

The Power of
BEING UNIQUE

The Power of
BEING UNIQUE

Power 32

The Power of Being Unique is all about being your true, authentic self.

> And it doesn't matter how different, or quirky or extreme that might be.

A lot of us spend way too much time trying to fit in, trying to be like someone else.

> There is this desire to be liked and to be loved as well as this fear that people won't like, love, or understand us if we just show up as ourselves.

But how boring would it be if we were all the same?

> Realize that your true value is just showing up as you.

If others like it, awesome. If others don't, that's okay.

> This week, think about your unique style. What is it about you that is different and special?

And when you figure it out, let it shine. Don't dim your light. Nobody can do you better than you.

Week of
_____

QUESTIONS TO CONSIDER

1. How did I apply this power this week?

2. How was my life changed/improved/better for using this power?

3. How will I move forward with this particular power?

NOTES

___	**SUNDAY**
___	**MONDAY**
___	**TUESDAY**
___	**WEDNESDAY**

TO-DO-LIST

THURSDAY

FRIDAY

SATURDAY

I am using the **POWER** of
Being Unique

The Power of
RECOGNIZING YOUR OWN IMPERFECTIONS

The Power of RECOGNIZING YOUR OWN IMPERFECTIONS

Power 33

The Power of Recognizing Your Own Imperfections is about looking at your words, thoughts and actions first before you start judging those around you.

> For example, when my two kids get into an argument, they immediately want to tell me all about what the other person did wrong.

And my immediate response to them is, "We'll get to that in a second. What did YOU do?"

> When you start with the role that you played in a particular disagreement, fuss or situation, it makes it a little bit easier to then understand what the other person did or didn't do. It makes it a little bit harder to be as critical and/or judgmental toward the other person.

Because at the end of the day, you cannot change that other person and what they said or did but you can do a whole lot about your own thoughts, words and actions.

> This week, think about a past argument you may have had and ask yourself the above question to get a better understanding of what took place. Or, if something comes up this week, take a step back and look at yourself and your role before jumping to any conclusions about the other person.

Week of
_____

QUESTIONS TO CONSIDER

1. How did I apply this power this week?

2. How was my life changed/improved/better for using this power?

3. How will I move forward with this particular power?

NOTES

SUNDAY

MONDAY

TUESDAY

WEDNESDAY

TO-DO-LIST

THURSDAY

FRIDAY

SATURDAY

I am using the **POWER** of
Recognizing Your Own Imperfections

The Power of
SOMETHING DIFFERENT

The Power of
SOMETHING DIFFERENT

Power 34

The Power of Something Different is all about your willingness to try something different, to be different.

> As children, with a lot of things, we were fearless. All someone had to do was dare us, or double dare us, and we were off and running.

However, at some point, we allowed fear to creep in. We became comfortable and content with things being predictable and the same. And now we wonder why we are bored or dissatisfied with our lives.

> But this is where this power is helpful.

In fact, when we are willing to experience different things, that's how our brains grow. That's how our knowledge expands. That's how we are able to say, "We know a little something about this or that."

> It can be as simple as trying a different food or cologne, or as big as dating a different type of guy or girl. Stop assuming that everything different will lead to a bad experience. You just might surprise yourself.

This week, try at least three different things, big or small, and just see how it feels and what you experience. You might just find a new favorite food or even your soulmate. You never know until you try.

Week of

_____

QUESTIONS TO CONSIDER

1. How did I apply this power this week?

2. How was my life changed/improved/better for using this power?

3. How will I move forward with this particular power?

NOTES

SUNDAY

MONDAY

TUESDAY

WEDNESDAY

TO-DO-LIST

THURSDAY

FRIDAY

SATURDAY

I am using the **POWER** of **Something Different**

The Power of
MY GIFT

The Power of
MY GIFT

Power 35

Every single solitary person has their own gift to share with the world, their own superpower.

> Unfortunately, a lot of us go through life not realizing this fact and even worse, never using it.

Often the world bombards us with so much negativity that our gifts get lost in the shuffle.

> Also, the worst negative talk often comes from ourselves.

This power counters all of that by first realizing that we have a gift and then spending time figuring out what it is.

> Then, it becomes easy and fun to actually use this gift.

This week, spend some time thinking about what your gift is. What is the thing that you do naturally? What is the thing that everyone seems to notice about you and compliments you on? How do you or how can you use that gift?

Week of
_____

QUESTIONS TO CONSIDER

1 How did I apply this power this week?

2 How was my life changed/improved/better for using this power?

3 How will I move forward with this particular power?

NOTES

____ **SUNDAY**

____ **MONDAY**

____ **TUESDAY**

____ **WEDNESDAY**

TO-DO-LIST

THURSDAY

FRIDAY

SATURDAY

I am using the **POWER** of
My Gift

The Power of PREPARATION

The Power of PREPARATION

Power 36

"Preparation, preparation, preparation" is a statement my former boss would always say.

> It took a while for me to fully understand the importance of it but now I see it clearly.

The Power of Preparation is about controlling as much as you can ahead of time, so that the latter part or execution of it is more efficient and streamlined.

> The more prepared you are regarding something, the more confident you will be in its execution.

It can be as simple as laying your clothes out the night before so you won't be as rushed and as frantic in the morning, or as complex as preparing for trial, as I used to do when practicing law.

> Preparation applies to both the biggest and smallest of tasks.

Just a few minutes of preparation can really make the difference, even when your plans change and you have to pivot.

> This week, prepare for something that you would normally just do on the fly and see the difference for yourself.

Week of
_____

QUESTIONS TO CONSIDER

1. How did I apply this power this week?

2. How was my life changed/improved/better for using this power?

3. How will I move forward with this particular power?

NOTES

___ SUNDAY

___ MONDAY

___ TUESDAY

___ WEDNESDAY

TO-DO-LIST

THURSDAY

FRIDAY

SATURDAY

I am using the **POWER** of
Preparation

The Power of
MONDAY DREAD

The Power of
MONDAY DREAD

Power 37

Monday Dread is when on Sunday, you realize that the weekend is nearly over and you have to face your job or some task, or someone that you do NOT want to face.

> This is a normal feeling to have every once in a while, but if it is the rule and not the exception, this power is for you.

The Power of the Monday Dread is paying attention to this feeling that you are having every single week and using it as an opportunity to learn something and make a change.

> What is causing you to feel this way? Is it something that just needs to be tweaked or does it need a complete overhaul? How can it be altered? How do you get rid of it?

These are all questions you can ask yourself to get to a happier state of mind.

> If this applies to you, let this week be the week that you examine the above and figure out a game plan to address it.

Week of

_____

QUESTIONS TO CONSIDER

1. How did I apply this power this week?

2. How was my life changed/improved/better for using this power?

3. How will I move forward with this particular power?

NOTES

SUNDAY

MONDAY

TUESDAY

WEDNESDAY

TO-DO-LIST

THURSDAY

FRIDAY

SATURDAY

I am using the **POWER** of
Monday Dread

The Power of
MY "HAVE TOS"

The Power of
MY "HAVE TOS"

Power 38

A "have to" is something that you HAVE TO do. For instance, you have to take care of your kids, or you have to help your parents, or you have to work.

> You can easily find out what your "have tos" are because they are all of the things that you will make sure get done no matter what.

In order to make The Power of Your Have Tos work for you, you must apply it to things that you don't always apply it to, like yourself. Apply it to your own self care, your own mental health, your own goals and dreams.

> Often times, we put ourselves on the back burner as something we will get around to when we have more time, more money, less obligations, etc.

Make yourself a "have to." Don't put YOU off. Do it now. Make it mandatory, not optional.

> This week, pick one thing that you have been putting off that is beneficial to you exclusively and make it a "have to."

Week of
_____

QUESTIONS TO CONSIDER

1 How did I apply this power this week?

2 How was my life changed/improved/better for using this power?

3 How will I move forward with this particular power?

NOTES

_____	**SUNDAY**

_____	**MONDAY**

_____	**TUESDAY**

_____	**WEDNESDAY**

TO-DO-LIST

THURSDAY

FRIDAY

SATURDAY

I am using the **POWER** of
My "Have Tos"

The Power of EVOLUTION

The Power of EVOLUTION

Power 39

The Power of Evolution is about giving yourself the opportunity to evolve, believing that you can be something different, and doing something different.

> You can change; you can create a new habit, or stop an old one.

You can pretty much evolve into whatever it is that you are trying to become if you can just stop limiting yourself.

> Often times, we can't meet expectations, goals, or dreams because we put ourselves in this box in terms of what we think we can do.

Sometimes, this is based upon something that happened in the past or our worry of what others will think.

> But the truth of the matter is that every day we have a chance to wake up and be different, if we choose.

You have a chance every day to learn something new, to grow, to change, to make a decision, to change your mind, to change again, - to evolve.

> This week, just think about the limitations that you've placed upon yourself. Are they based upon facts? Are they true? Are they excuses to stay in the same space? How much more could you experience if you removed just one?

Week of

_____

QUESTIONS TO CONSIDER

1. How did I apply this power this week?

2. How was my life changed/improved/better for using this power?

3. How will I move forward with this particular power?

NOTES

| _____ | **SUNDAY** |

| _____ | **MONDAY** |

| _____ | **TUESDAY** |

| _____ | **WEDNESDAY** |

TO-DO-LIST

THURSDAY

FRIDAY

SATURDAY

I am using the **POWER** of

Evolution

The Power of
WORST-CASE SCENARIO/ LIFE EXPERIENCE

The Power of
WORST-CASE SCENARIO/
LIFE EXPERIENCE

Power 40

The Power of the Worst-Case Scenario/Life Experience is having the ability to look at something that has occurred in your life that was not good and choosing to be better as opposed to bitter because of it.

> Often times, when something bad happens to us, we allow ourselves to get upset which is normal.

Sometimes, though, we don't stop there; we let the bad experience consume us and before we know it, we become bitter and we allow that bitterness to grow and expand into all kinds of areas of our lives.

> We don't have to do this; we have a choice.

We can choose to be bitter and carry all of the baggage that comes along with bitterness OR we can choose to learn from that experience and actually be better because of it.

> Now this may not apply to all bad things that happen to us but for most of them, it does.

This week, think about something bad that happened to you in the past and reflect on how you handled it. Did you allow yourself to be bitter? If so, how can you now turn it around? What lesson can you learn from it, even now, to change your path from bitterness to becoming better?

Week of

_____

QUESTIONS TO CONSIDER

1. How did I apply this power this week?

2. How was my life changed/improved/better for using this power?

3. How will I move forward with this particular power?

NOTES

SUNDAY

MONDAY

TUESDAY

WEDNESDAY

TO-DO-LIST

THURSDAY

FRIDAY

SATURDAY

I am using the **POWER** of the
Worst-Case Scenario/ Life Experience

The Power of
HANDLING DISTRACTION VAMPIRES

The Power of
HANDLING DISTRACTION VAMPIRES

Power 41

Distraction Vampires are anyone or anything that takes up your time when you are trying to do something else.

> Sometimes it's family and friends, or sometimes it's just us allowing ourselves to be distracted by emails, social media, etc. as opposed to being focused on the task at hand.

The power is in discerning when something or someone has become a distraction vampire and then, doing something about it.

> Distraction vampires happen to us day in and day out, sometimes without us being aware; they cause us to move at a slower pace than we should, or worse, we don't move at all.

And when you attempt to be productive while engaging the distraction vampire, you are in essence slowing both activities down and quite frankly, not performing either one of them very well.

> One solution to the vampire distraction is to either set rules or boundaries in place. For example, if your distraction vampire comes in the form of emails, texts, or phone calls from your phone during work hours, put the phone on silent, do not disturb, or at least shut off the pings and dings that occur with every notification. You can set a rule to not look at your phone unless you are on a break, at lunchtime, or after work.

Another solution is set boundaries when your distraction vampire shows up as a person. Let's say you are getting non-work related calls during work hours and you are trying to get something done. Just don't answer the phone OR inform whomever, that you can only talk at a certain time or that you will call them back when you are free. All of these are a form of boundary setting.

This week, what distraction vampire can you find in your life and what are some rules or boundaries you can put in place as to how you deal with him, her, or it? You'll be surprised as to how much extra time you can find by doing this one simple thing.

Week of
_____

QUESTIONS TO CONSIDER

1. How did I apply this power this week?

2. How was my life changed/improved/better for using this power?

3. How will I move forward with this particular power?

SUNDAY

MONDAY

TUESDAY

WEDNESDAY

NOTES

TO-DO-LIST

THURSDAY

FRIDAY

SATURDAY

I am using the **POWER** of
Handling Distraction Vampires

The Power of
TIME MANAGEMENT

The Power of TIME MANAGEMENT

Power 42

The Power of Time Management is the ability to put yourself in control of your time and not the other way around.

> Too often, we are simply moving around, like slaves to the master of time. We talk about how busy we are and what we would do if we had more time, blah blah blah. When in reality, with a few tweaks to our current schedule, we have enough time right now.

A lot of us, in fact, are wasting time and don't even realize it.

> There is a simple fix to this.

First, do a time study. It's nothing fancy but for 5-7 days, record what you are doing every waking hour of the day.

> Once that's complete, look at where most of your time is going. How much time is spent on things that you must do? Look closely at the items that you state MUST be done. Do they have to be done by you? Can the time it takes to do those items be reduced, delegated, or eliminated altogether?

Once you have done this and carved out some additional time, then look at your calendar from the standpoint of figuring out what it is you want to do. At this point, there should be gaps that you can fill in so that you are spending more time the way you want to.

> This week, try the above exercise and gain control of your time again.

Week of
_____

QUESTIONS TO CONSIDER

1. How did I apply this power this week?

2. How was my life changed/improved/better for using this power?

3. How will I move forward with this particular power?

NOTES

SUNDAY

MONDAY

TUESDAY

WEDNESDAY

TO-DO-LIST

THURSDAY

FRIDAY

SATURDAY

I am using the **POWER** of
Time Management

The Power of
BEING SICK & TIRED
OF BEING SICK & TIRED

The Power of
BEING SICK & TIRED OF BEING SICK & TIRED

Power 43

Sometimes we get sick and tired of being sick and tired. We hit rock bottom; we feel like we can't go any further. Sometimes, we must be pushed all the way to the edge of the cliff before we are willing to do something.

> This is The Power of Being Sick and Tired of Being Sick and Tired.

It's when we are at our breaking point and we cannot go one more day, but then we decide to do something different. We decide to make a change. We decide to ACT.

> I don't know why we wait until we get to that point to make moves but since we do, we should look at it as a resource, as potentially a good thing that we can then use to our advantage and harness that power.

This week, think about this, is there something that you are sick and tired of being sick and tired of? Is there something that you've been complaining about and talking about but not doing anything about? If so, now's a great time for you to really put some action behind that feeling. You don't have to be sick and tired. You can make a different choice. You CAN decide differently.

Week of

_____

QUESTIONS TO CONSIDER

1. How did I apply this power this week?

2. How was my life changed/improved/better for using this power?

3. How will I move forward with this particular power?

NOTES

SUNDAY

MONDAY

TUESDAY

WEDNESDAY

TO-DO-LIST

THURSDAY

FRIDAY

SATURDAY

I am using the **POWER** of

Being Sick and Tired of Being Sick and Tired

The Power of
TURNING PROBLEMS INTO SOLUTIONS

The Power of
TURNING PROBLEMS INTO SOLUTIONS

Power 44

The Power of Turning Problems into Solutions is all about shifting our mindset.

> Often, when we have a problem, we use up all of our time, energy, and attention on the problem.

We focus on the problem; we can't see past the problem; we are overwhelmed by the problem itself.

> Instead of focusing on the problem, we need to reframe the problem. For example, "I hate my job." The focus is on the job that I hate. I can't see past it when I think about it that way. However, if I reframe the problem to, "I'm going to look for new job opportunities," I have turned something that sucks the energy and life out of me into something that motivates me and gives me something to look forward to.

That's The Power of Turning Problems into Solutions. The issue hasn't changed but your mindset toward it makes all the difference and because of that shift, your situation will change.

> This week, look at just one area in your life that you have been defining as a problem. Start looking at it in a way that you can reframe that problem and come up with just one solution, one goal, one step toward that solution or goal to make that problem disappear. Before you know it, you no longer have a problem.

Week of

_____

QUESTIONS TO CONSIDER

1 How did I apply this power this week?

2 How was my life changed/improved/better for using this power?

3 How will I move forward with this particular power?

NOTES

SUNDAY

MONDAY

TUESDAY

WEDNESDAY

TO-DO-LIST

THURSDAY

FRIDAY

SATURDAY

I am using the **POWER** of
Turning Problems into Solutions

The Power of
THANKFULNESS

The Power of THANKFULNESS

Power 45

The Power of Thankfulness is not a new concept.

> It's when you consistently show gratitude for everything and anything you have in your life (your health, your family, the air you breathe, etc.).

The Power of Thankfulness is when you intentionally remember all of the things you need to be thankful for as opposed to getting caught up in all of the negative things that happen to you, or simply just happen.

> We can't turn on the news sometimes without seeing something that sends us down the path of negativity, anxiety and fear.

The Power of Thankfulness is a great way to counter that.

> This week, instead of getting up in the morning and immediately immersing yourself in gloom and doom, try getting up and writing in a gratitude journal 3-5 things that you are grateful for. Continue writing, if you want, by thinking of all of the things and people you feel that you take for granted. Commit to writing about it and showing gratitude for a period of time and just watch how things change.

Week of

_____

QUESTIONS TO CONSIDER

1. How did I apply this power this week?

2. How was my life changed/improved/better for using this power?

3. How will I move forward with this particular power?

NOTES

| _____ | **SUNDAY** |

| _____ | **MONDAY** |

| _____ | **TUESDAY** |

| _____ | **WEDNESDAY** |

TO-DO-LIST

THURSDAY

FRIDAY

SATURDAY

I am using the **POWER** of **Thankfulness**

The Power of
GENEROSITY

The Power of
GENEROSITY

Power 46

The Power of Generosity is simple; it is about being generous to others with your time, money, talent, and/or gifts.

> This power is about others. When you are generous with others, it indirectly comes back to you.

When you put something good out into the world, it does come back to you.

> So, the next time a friend, family member, or co-worker asks you to do something for them, consider doing it. Do it without hesitation or complaint. Or be proactive and find someone to be generous to. It could be the person behind you in the McDonald's line or if you're feeling especially generous, the person behind you in Target.

This week, incorporate generosity into your routine and watch it have an impact.

Week of
_____

QUESTIONS TO CONSIDER

1. How did I apply this power this week?

2. How was my life changed/improved/better for using this power?

3. How will I move forward with this particular power?

NOTES

SUNDAY

MONDAY

TUESDAY

WEDNESDAY

TO-DO-LIST

THURSDAY

FRIDAY

SATURDAY

I am using the **POWER** of **Generosity**

The Power of
KINDNESS

The Power of KINDNESS

Power 47

Kindness is a power that is often overlooked and underrated.

> Being kind doesn't cost you anything and yet sometimes it's hard to find.

But when it happens, it takes on a life of its own, especially for the person you are actually kind to.

> While people don't seem to value kindness or being kind as much as they used to, it's one of those things that will never go out of style.

Being kind to family members and friends, even strangers, can often have a ripple effect that you as the person being kind, may never see. But trust me, it's there.

> So be kind, even when you don't want to, even if you question whether the other person deserves it. You never know what someone is going through at that precise moment in time. You never know how God may be using you in that one moment to shift someone's mindset, to help someone, to just be a positive force in the world.

This week, be kind. It may not change your life, but it will definitely have a positive effect on someone else's.

Week of

_____

QUESTIONS TO CONSIDER

1. How did I apply this power this week?

2. How was my life changed/improved/better for using this power?

3. How will I move forward with this particular power?

NOTES

	SUNDAY

	MONDAY

	TUESDAY

	WEDNESDAY

TO-DO-LIST

THURSDAY

FRIDAY

SATURDAY

I am using the **POWER** of

Kindness

The Power of
THE
NEVER ENDING TRY

The Power of
THE NEVER ENDING TRY

Power 48

The Power of the Never-Ending Try is when you try, you try, and you try again. You don't stop trying until you get to whatever it is you are wanting to accomplish.

> A lot of times we look at successful people and think that they have some sort of extraordinary gift or talent that allows them to accomplish a certain thing and we distinguish ourselves from them because of it.

And often they do have a gift or talent but the real difference between us and them is that they decided to keep trying.

> The average person may try a certain thing 10 times and these people that we look up to were willing to try it 100 times.

It's not that they had something we didn't have, they just didn't give up.

> Now, there may be some things that we just aren't cut out to do; however, for the majority of our dreams and goals, this is applicable.

This week, really look at something you are trying to accomplish that you are just about ready to give up on. Really sit down and consider whether you've given it your all. You may just be right at the brink of success if you're willing to give it a couple more tries!

Week of

_____

QUESTIONS TO CONSIDER

1. How did I apply this power this week?

2. How was my life changed/improved/better for using this power?

3. How will I move forward with this particular power?

NOTES

| _____ | **SUNDAY** |

| _____ | **MONDAY** |

| _____ | **TUESDAY** |

| _____ | **WEDNESDAY** |

TO-DO-LIST

THURSDAY

FRIDAY

SATURDAY

I am using the **POWER** of
The Never-Ending Try

The Power of YOU

The Power of YOU

Power 49

I want to focus on you for a moment and talk about The Power of You. The Power of You is about taking the negative self-talk and substituting positive energy.

> You ARE important. You ARE strong. You ARE capable. You ARE loving. You ARE kind.

A lot of us don't hear that often enough from others; more importantly, we don't tell it to ourselves.

> But it is time to start looking at yourself, loving yourself, and believing these things about yourself.

You are stronger than you realize. You are more capable. You are intelligent. You can do anything that you put your mind to. You just must start with the belief in yourself.

> This week, every morning, before you get caught up in the hustle and bustle of life, just talk to yourself for a minute. You can do it while still in the bed with your eyes closed or standing in a wonder woman pose (feet apart and hands on hips) in front of the mirror. Whatever works for you.

Week of
_____

QUESTIONS TO CONSIDER

1 How did I apply this power this week?

2 How was my life changed/improved/better for using this power?

3 How will I move forward with this particular power?

NOTES

____ **SUNDAY**

____ **MONDAY**

____ **TUESDAY**

____ **WEDNESDAY**

TO-DO-LIST

THURSDAY

FRIDAY

SATURDAY

I am using the **POWER** of
You

The Power of REST

The Power of REST

Power 50

The Power of Rest is simple. It's incorporating time to just be, instead of always concerning yourself with what you are doing.

> The importance of rest is underestimated. Often, we believe that in order to obtain our goals, we must be busy at all times; we must be working hard all the time; we must be on the go, all of the time.

That is simply not the case.

> Rest and work go hand and hand; they are part of the same cycle.

It's not that you can't meet your goals by working yourself to death; you can. But, if you decide to do it that way, your success will be short-lived. At some point, your mind, body and soul won't allow you to continue to sustain it, if you continue to cut rest out of the equation.

> This week, incorporate more rest into your schedule. Whether it's making sure you get 8 hours of sleep or just incorporating a 10-15 minute power nap into your day. Just don't burn the candle at both ends this week and see how it feels. You just might have a breakthrough during those periods of rest this week.

Week of

_____

QUESTIONS TO CONSIDER

1. How did I apply this power this week?

2. How was my life changed/improved/better for using this power?

3. How will I move forward with this particular power?

NOTES

SUNDAY

MONDAY

TUESDAY

WEDNESDAY

TO-DO-LIST

THURSDAY

FRIDAY

SATURDAY

I am using the **POWER** of

Rest

The Power of
THE TIME WE HAVE LEFT

The Power of
THE TIME WE HAVE LEFT

Power 51

The Power of the Time We Have Left is about focusing on your future as opposed to looking backwards in the rearview mirror at everything that has already taken place.

> Too often, we get stuck in the past and live in the present with baggage and regret and desires to change outcomes that have already occurred.

While there is nothing wrong with reminiscing and having memories about our past, it is problematic when we choose to stay there in our minds and no longer live in the present or plan for our future.

> Our past happened and we can't change it. But what we can change is the effects it has on us today.

Time moves on whether we are stuck or not and one day we will run out of it.

> This week, focus on the now and the future. Focus on what's next and LIVE!

Week of

_____

QUESTIONS TO CONSIDER

1. How did I apply this power this week?

2. How was my life changed/improved/better for using this power?

3. How will I move forward with this particular power?

NOTES

SUNDAY

_____
_____
_____
_____
_____

MONDAY

_____
_____
_____
_____
_____

TUESDAY

_____
_____
_____
_____
_____

WEDNESDAY

_____
_____
_____
_____
_____

TO-DO-LIST

THURSDAY

FRIDAY

SATURDAY

I am using the **POWER** of the
Time We Have Left

The Power of
NOW

The Power of NOW

Power 52

The Power of Now is realizing that NOW is the only real measure of time that matters.

> When we focus on the past, we tend to get stuck in "woulda coulda shoulda land," and when we focus too much on the future, we can get caught up in over analyzing and spending too much time on "what if" scenarios that never happen.

Since we don't control either the past or the future, we should just stay in the lane of what we can control, the NOW.

> NOW is also a good place to start doing things.

We don't need to wait until later, until the kids go to college, until we retire, until we drop "x" amount of pounds.

> Stop putting off those things and penciling them in for later. What if later never comes?

How would your life be different if you started now?

> This week, think about the one thing that you've been putting off. What is the one thing that you can take off your "to do later" list and do NOW? Once you figure it out, DO IT. NOW.

Week of

_____

QUESTIONS TO CONSIDER

1 How did I apply this power this week?

2 How was my life changed/improved/better for using this power?

3 How will I move forward with this particular power?

NOTES

SUNDAY

MONDAY

TUESDAY

WEDNESDAY

TO-DO-LIST

THURSDAY

FRIDAY

SATURDAY

I am using the **POWER** of
Now

Thank you so much for allowing me to share in your personal development journey. I hope that you were able to find value each week with each power that was shared and that your life has noticeably changed for the better since first embarking on this journey a year ago. Feel free to drop a line to me on my facebook business page or check me out at www.thelifechangercoach.com for additional helpful tools. I'd love to assist you as you continue your journey of becoming the best version of yourself and accomplishing your dreams and goals, one week at a time!

Take care,
Danese – The Life Changer Coach

ABOUT THE AUTHOR

Danese Banks is the founder and CEO of The Life Changer Coach, LLC. She is both a Certified Professional Coach and Energy Leadership Index Master Practitioner. She spends her time coaching people whose inner blocks and obstacles have gotten in the way of achieving their outer goals, particularly those she refers to as "deferred dreamers". In her "previous career life", she was the Managing Partner of the Memphis office at The Cochran Firm, founded by the late Johnnie L. Cochran, Jr. She has been an attorney for over twenty-five years and still uses her "legal brain" as a mediator in her separate business, Banks Mediation Services.

Both jobs provide her with the opportunity to serve people in the way she loves best, by solving problems and resolving conflict. When she's not doing either job, she enjoys, walking, dancing, being silly with her husband, two children and fur baby, traveling, and shopping. She plans on writing children's books one day in her future. You can learn more about her at www.thelifechangercoach.com and www.banksmediationservices.com.